CENTURY END

A FLY TYING JOURNEY

SOME ORIGINALS
SOME TRADITIONALS
SOME OBSERVATIONS

PAUL PTALIS

Frank Amato
PORTLAND

DEDICATION

RALPH AND EVELYN PTALIS

MY DEVOTED PARENTS

JOHN WEAVER
1942-1999
A FINE FLY TIER AND FRIEND

Published in 2000 by Frank Amato Publications, Inc.
P.O. Box 82112, Portland, Oregon 97282
(503) 653-8108 www.amatobooks.com

All flies tied by the author.

ISBN: 1-57188-218-9
UPC: 0-66066-00432-1

Printed in Singapore by Star Standard Industries (Pte) Ltd.

10 9 8 7 6 5 4 3 2 1

Contents

Acknowledgements.. 7

Introduction.. 8

Color and Flow.. 11

Patterns:

99 Pure... 18

African Gray... 19

The Bronze Pirate 6/0.................................. 20

The Bronze Pirate #4................................... 21

Blue Capped Macaw Chatterer Variation......................... 22

Kingfisher Chatterer Variation 23

Red Capped Lori Chatterer Variation 24

Red Cheeked Macaw Chatterer Variation........................ 25

Sun Conour Chatterer Variation....................... 26

Eck's Engine... 27

Elliot's... 28

The Emerald Peacock..................................... 29

Evan's Fancy.. 30

Floodtide.. 31

Green Highlander... 32

Grey Eagle.. 33

Harmony... 34

Ibis & Mearns.. 35

JK's Fault.. 36

Justin's Fancy.. 37

Moon and Stars... 38

The Popham 1996.. 39

The Popham 1998.. 40

Primary Direction.. 41

Regal King.. 42

Roy G Biv... 43

Sarah's Fancy.. 44

The Scarlet Gem.. 45

Scarlet Queen... 46

Shewey's Marabou Blue................................. 47

Spring Fancy... 48

Tippetiwitchet... 49

The Torrish... 50

Yellow Eagle... 51

HOOKS...52

   ANTIQUE:

      R. WILLIS & SONS CIRCA 1920 BRONZE JAPANNED............ 54

      WM. BARTLEET & SONS FINE WIRE LIMERICK.................... 55

      R. HARRISON CELEBRATED DUBLIN LIMERICK..................... 56

      WM. BARTLEET & SONS LIMERICK.................................. 56

      R. HARRISON BARTLEET & CO.

          CELEBRATED SPRING STEEL SPROAT......................... 57

      PENNELL'S SPROAT X HEAVY WIRE............................... 57

      ADLINGTON ROUND BEND... 57

      H. MILLWARD LIMERICK... 58

      LOW WATER SALMON HOOK CIRCA PRE-WWII................. 58

      EDGAR SEALEY & SONS HOLLOW POINT SPROAT............. 59

      FRANCIS FRANCIS PLATE 13 CARLISLE BEND.................... 59

      ALLCOCK LIMERICK.. 59

      R. HARRISON BARTLEET & CO. LIMERICK....................... 60

      HARRISON BARTLEET'S HOLLOW POINT SPROAT BEND...... 60

      MUSTAD #3450.. 60

      MUSTAD #3899.. 61

   CONTEMPORARY HOOKS OF R.W. REINHOLD...................... 62

      WM. BARTLEET & SONS... 63

      HARRISON HOLLOW POINT... 64

      NOBLE HB... 64

      PHILLIPS LIMERICK.. 65

      NOBLE P... 65

      WM. BARTLEET... 66

      DROUGHTWATER DEE 66

      T.E. PRYCE-TANNATT GROUP A 67

      HARRISON BARTLEET 67

      MILWARD BARTLEET... 67

      NOBLE S... 68

   CONTEMPORARY HOOKS OF RAY SMITH 69

      WM. BARTLEET & SONS LIMERICK 70

      WM. BARTLEET LIMERICK 71

      HARRISON CELEBRATED LIMERICK 71

      PHILLIPS OF DUBLIN 72

      PRYCE-TANNATT RATIONAL.. 72

CONTEMPORARY HOOKS OF EUGENE SUNDAY.................... 73
    WM. BARTLEET & SONS LIMERICK.................................. 74
    MADDEN CELEBRATED LIMERICK.. 75
    HARRISON HOLLOW POINT LIMERICK................................ 75
    MILLWARD 76
    MATTHEW'S SUPERFINE FORGED IRON............................ 76
NOTES.. 77

ACKNOWLEDGEMENTS

Special Thanks:

Marilyn - my wife, my friend, for her unwavering support for this project. Especially for pretending to ignore those packages (of special materials) that mysteriously appeared at our doorstep from time to time.

Evan and Sarah - my children, for their patience and inspiration. They grew up doing their schoolwork at an adjacent desk to my fly tying bench. For allowing me to review their homework and give advise in between tying flies.

Fred Clason - my special friend, who introduced me to the world of fly-fishing and tying. I wouldn't be enjoying myself in this way if it weren't for him.

Jim Krul and Al Coif - for their friendship and encouragement, the depth of their knowledge was always there for me, "on call" and on an emergency basis.

Mike Martinek Jr. and Max MacPherson Jr. - your lessons did not go to waste.

Ron Reinhold - for the best modern hooks available today, you're truly an artist.

Paul Schmookler - you never hesitate to advise, critique and share your expertise. Your creativity is an inspiration to all of us.

Jordan Stitzer - a friend whose editing brought order to my writing.

Special thanks to the myriad of **Salmon Fly Tiers** who share their techniques, secrets, attitudes and resources.

To my mother, **Evelyn**, for teaching me to look for artistic "line" and "flow," and encouraging me to be creative.

INTRODUCTION

Salmon fly tying is my obsession. I make no bones about it, as I'm in very good company. Those who tie these flies know what I mean. Those who are on the verge of beginning the journey have already felt the visual exhilaration these magnificent flies exude. Their beauty and attraction, for me at least, developed after a long period of tying the usual trout flies.

I started tying the most common, versatile patterns, which included an Adams #12, a Hare's Ear Nymph #12, a Mickey Finn #6, and a Black Ghost #6, and quickly learned to tie other fly patterns in a variety of sizes. I was off and running, tying over 300 flies before hooking my first fish. While fly-fishing became a real love of mine, fly tying dwarfed all my other angling interests. It was more than just a winter diversion or the mandatory preparation anticipating next season. I just love tying flies!

Soon my fly fishing travels took me to the Lake Ontario tributaries for Steelhead and Salmon. There I learned to tie with synthetics, the politically correct term for plastic. It was truly amazing how these gaudy, fluorescent flies tied in the traditional streamer and nymph silhouettes, attracted these huge fish. I started developing my own patterns in which color was an appropriate and successful infinite variable, any colors you liked, any combinations. I must have tied thousands of these flies, more than could be used in one's lifetime.

My interest in Steelhead fishing expanded. I became interested in Steelhead flies, fishing and fly tying techniques from the Northwest. I then discovered the "Spey Fly" and the need for a whole new world of materials. This was the beginning of the obsession, although I didn't know it yet. This leg of my journey started out simple enough, goose quill secondaries, spey hackles, silk and dubbing, a blue eared pheasant (heron substitute) was a must as I was catapulted into "3 figure" materials. And the new techniques; folding hackles and mounting the flimsy wings of goose secondaries.

Consistent with my approach to most things in which I become interested, and more specifically, my focus on fly tying, I began to explore the history of the spey fly. This put me on yet another road, across the continent, across the Atlantic, to England, Ireland and Scotland and back in time beyond the last Century End when the original Spey and Classic Atlantic Salmon flies were originated and flourished as "fishing" flies.

What can I say, Francis Francis, Kelson, Pryce-Tannatt, Jones, etc., I fell in love with the Classic Atlantic Salmon Fly and became possessed by the color, line, and flow of these flies. Of particular interest and curiosity to me was the challenge of the underlying techniques and tier's skills that needed to be employed to achieve what I considered to be "works of art."

I continued on my journey, reading every book I could find on tying classic salmon flies, books written by the masters of the 1800's as well as modern masters. In these books I found a plethora of information and began collecting antique hooks and replicas of these hooks made by contemporary "masters." I also collected quality materials, which would be used at a later date when I felt my tying skills were worthy. Although I did as much tying as I could, something was missing. Lessons to learn how to handle materials and tying Carrie Stevens streamers was the right choice for me. Learning left wing from right wing, curve up, curve down, and the most important lesson - "if the materials don't want to work together, all the manipulation in the world won't make them want to work together, choose another hackle!"

I also took one-on-one classic salmon tying lessons concentrating on basic techniques; married wing, full-feather wing, dubbed body, silk body, crests and hackle. In this way the Master focused fully and intensely on what I needed. I continued to tie, but still, something was missing. I tied much better salmon flies by this point, but they weren't perfect. I wasn't satisfied.

I started to go to the fly shows and talk to every salmon tier about their flies and my flies when I had the courage and thought the time was right. Although some tiers were more outgoing than others, they all answered my questions and even sometimes shared, what seemed to me, their most guarded secret techniques. I began to realize that here lied the answer to my dissatisfaction with my flies. Most writers and teachers related their own techniques, the ones that worked for them. They didn't write about how it felt to use one technique versus another technique. This was the issue. I was trying to exactly duplicate, both from a technical and a visual perspective, someone else's work. While I had gained skills, I hadn't developed my own techniques, the ones that were personal to me. I therefore hadn't yet developed my own style. I wasn't thinking outside the box!

So why this book?

I am trying to relate my opinions regarding "thinking outside the box" to other tiers, especially the newcomers. Being conscious about several facets of the salmon fly that are usually not considered until after its completion, if at all. I hope the reader will benefit from my own observations and opinions, most of which have not appeared in the literature although certainly talked about amongst the tiers. For me this includes a heavy reliance on the natural beauty of the materials and their combinations and placement on the hook, especially when designing one's own fly. Hence, the discussion about "seeing the materials." Another important facet involves "flow." To me this concept provides movement to a static object. It helps a fly "work" artistically. Hence, the discussion about "flow."

I have also included two sections illustrating hooks from antique and contemporary hook makers. While these sections don't purport to be all inclusive, they do provide a varied selection of size, bend style, and point style. Most of the visual resources available today merely represent the hook as a silhouette rather that an actual-size photographic representation. I felt this would be of value to the novice salmon tier as well as those with more experience who may already have a large hook collection. Hopefully, in the near future, someone will write a book devoted to the history of antique hooks, illustrated with graphic representations.

Lastly, I want to document and share some of my original and traditional flies. It is important to me to leave this legacy for my children and their families.

Paul Ptalis
Cheshire, Connecticut
October 1999

COLOR AND FLOW
"SEEING" THE MATERIALS

The history surrounding the Classic Atlantic Salmon Fly is rich with tradition and followed by many in a purist fashion. The classic books, written by Kelson, Pryce-Tannatt, Hale, etc., document patterns in a very distinct manner. They lead one to believe, especially those new to the subject, that each fly must be tied in a specific manner and with a very exacting result. Is this Baron tied correctly? Does it look the way it is supposed to look? While this line of questioning is appropriate, as we learn the basics, it inevitably hinders our ability to "think outside the box," and make progress towards developing one's own style. To me, the development of one's own style and the confidence in that style is the single most important aspect of salmon fly tying. Style is the essence of one's progression towards the art form, of gaining another level of enjoyment in tying these flies and appreciating the flies tied by others.

Whether tying classic salmon flies using traditional patterns or designing one's own patterns, several aspects of the process become more important if the flies are to be mounted for exhibition and viewed as an art form. While fishing flies are beautiful objects in themselves, they are designed more for the way they will function in the water than their form. There are many superb books available that cover the "How To's" of salmon fly tying. However, very few touch the subject of color and flow. The following sections will briefly touch upon these facets of form. They are very personal as each of us "sees" and reacts to color, line, and movement differently. Therefore, the following observations are intended to tweak one's imagination and consciousness while contemplating their own creations.

🪰 Traditional salmon fly patterns call for feathers that are extremely beautiful in terms of color and texture. Many of these materials are either no longer available or are too expensive. However, many other materials are available, many of which are equally as colorful and interesting as the classic materials. One just needs to spend the time "seeing" the materials to recognize their potential.

🪰 "Seeing" the material will unlock their characteristics. For example; delicacy, overall color, graduating color (usually from butt to tip of feather), size, perimeter shape, bend of feather (up, down), concaveness, width, length, overall feather line, center stem line, pattern or mottling, thickness of fibers, texture, stiffness, iridescence, etc.

❧ "Seeing" the characteristics of other materials is equally as important. For example, shape of the hook bend, shape of the hook point, length of the hook shank, width of the hook gape, thickness of the silk gut, texture of the gut (number of twisted fibers), texture of the floss (silk, rayon, nylon etc.), depth of floss color, color of tinsel (more gold content, less gold content), etc.

❧ Combining several of these characteristics in the right proportion, line, shape and color can be very powerful in creating a fly that "works."

❧ Look at materials that are not called for in the traditional patterns. Think about how you could use their characteristics rather than wondering if they are "required" for a specific pattern. How many times have I heard someone say, "I don't need parakeet feathers, there are no patterns that call for them." However, parakeet feathers are readily available, they are magnificently colored, and they can be easily used in a variety of ways. For example, as cheeks, body veiling as in a chatterer variation (see pages 16-20), and the larger under-tail coverts can be used on the body under the shank such as on Evan's and Sarah's Fancy (see pages 24 and 38 respectively).

❧ Under-tail coverts are one of my favorite feathers. Magnificent specimens can be found on Lorikeets, Macaws, Parrots, many pheasants, Rosellas, Parakeets, etc. Most birds yield about 5 or 6 pairs of under-tail coverts in graduating sizes. The three pairs of green-tipped red feathers on Evan's Fancy (see page 24) is an example of how magnificent these feathers can be. The down side comes with respect to duplicating a fly tied with these feathers. Each bird comes with their own unique coloring. The chances of finding two birds with the exact same markings on their under-tail coverts is sometimes not possible. As in the case of Evan's Fancy, I was only able to tie two of these flies.

❧ Look at a feather from all angles. Look for hidden color. Many feathers have iridescence to them which may reveal a unique characteristic that would otherwise have gone without being noticed. For example, the green wing in Sarah's Fancy is an under-tail covert from a large macaw. The feather is light green and when held at an angle to reflect light off its surface reveals a marked blue-green tinge. This led me to match up a Kenya Crested Guinea

Fowl for the shoulder. The Kenya Crested is known for its subtle blue "half moon" in each white dot of its body feathers. My thought was even though one could not see the blue in the green wing (looking straight on), it is still there. Let's say its subliminally there. I thought the Kenya Crested blue would be a great complement to the wing. I was right, it worked.

Guinea fowl come in many varieties and are not expensive. They have some very useful characteristics; they are patterned with white dots and they come with a variety of background colors. When used as a shoulder they provide a foreground color that complements the wing color. Examples of this can be seen in the African Gray and Ibis & Mearns on pages 13 and 29 respectively. On smaller flies these feathers can be used as throats to complement a variety of situations.

Another approach is to consider using several feathers from the same bird (see The Bronze Pirate on pages 14 and 15). They will definitely work together. My theory behind this is; God created these beautiful creatures, He created feathers of different colors on the same bird, if it worked for Him, it will work for me. It did for Kelson!

Look to nature for inspiration. Red, yellow and blue are the primary colors. They will always work together (see Primary Direction on page 35).

I do not mean to over-simplify the elements necessary to create an artistic salmon fly. However, I believe that by breaking down these facets to their simplest expression, one can more easily appreciate the value of maintaining them in consciousness while creating the fly and achieve better outcomes.

Natural or dyed materials? I always prefer natural materials because the colors are always more complex. A dyed red feather is red. A natural red feather has a variety of reds, usually more saturated and intense. The fibers are softer, not having gone through the dying process. I no longer use dyed black ostrich herl. I find black dye is a harsh color, often with an unnatural green iridescent tinge. Natural ostrich herl, charcoal gray, is softer looking and contributes more to the flow of color. Likewise, I do not use dyed black turkey tail fibers. I favor Capercaillie tail fibers for their softer, more natural look (see Roy G Biv on page 37).

🦟 Look at traditional patterns from your own creative perspective. Kelson and Pryce-Tannatt did. Many of the patterns they published differed considerably in the construction of the wing as well as the materials used. The two Popham flies (on pages 33 and 34) illustrate this attitude. While they use the identical materials they look like two different flies. The materials used in their wings are constructed in different order and the flows of the flies vary considerably. Same fly, different approach. Think outside the box, it's OK.

🦟 The "flow" of a fly gives it movement through extension. The lines should extend past the materials to form some imagined closure. This is where the characteristics of the hook, crests, throat, and shape of the wing can play a very dramatic role. It is the overall flow and line extension of the fly that I am seeking. I Plan the fly's construction well in advance. For instance, it is important for me to imagine the resulting flow of the throat through the hook point as I choose the curve of the tail crest that will complement the wing and top crest. This may seem a bit contrived or complicated. But for me it is the way I think about tying my classic salmon flies and really quite simple.

The flow of the throat in relation to the hook point is
supported by the flow of the stems of the feathers under
the hook shank.

🦟 The following illustrations are not intended as instructions. They are shown to illustrate what I think about as I tie a fly and attempt to achieve a pleasing feeling about its visual aspects. This is a very individualized approach. One should not try to replicate what I have done with my flies as much as think about these concepts and create the flow that is personally pleasing to the tier.

 A dramatically different approach to the throat is illustrated in the Green Highlander below. In order to achieve a graduated effect of the hackle and dubbing from the throat back to the silk, the throat is tied in straight. The backward angle of the throat is complemented by the angle of the tinsel ribbing. Additionally, the wing is kept low and tight to the hook shank and is complemented by a hollow point. I find the hollow point hooks complement the line of the crests whereas a Dublin point complements a curved throat.

The oval tinsel complements the throat line.

The crescent moon shape of the hollow point complements the line of the tail and top crests.

Movement is another important dimension of flow. I find employing symmetry, tying-in materials at coordinated angles and seeing intersecting lines of extension useful in achieving a "non-static" fly.

The body veiling is tied in at a dramatic angle. Their butts complement the throat line while their extended lines run counter to and intersect the extended throat line. The "crest capsule" is exaggerated which also contributes to this fly's "flow."

The use of symmetric curved and straight lines of flow emanating from the head (starting point of direction) helps achieve movement. The horns complement the "crest capsule." The compressed tail veiling and parallel wing stem also add to the flow.

 All things meet in the end. Sometimes literally and sometimes through lines of extension, but there is always closure.

The stems of all the wing feathers line-up with the terminal ends of the crests. This needs to be planned from the very beginning.

........from a philosophical perspective -

The essence of any object (material) can only be understood if we "see" it from all possible aspects at the same time, which is impossible for us to do. The next best thing is to "see" it from *as many aspects* as we can at one time. Therefore, look at the materials, look at the flow. Train yourself to be conscious of these things, as "you" see them, while your tying. You will increase your confidence, realize better outcomes, and eventually develop your own style.

99 Pure
Designed & Tied by Paul Ptalis 1992

HOOK:	6/0 STERLING SILVER, DESIGNED BY PAUL PTALIS
TAG:	FINE SILVER OVAL TINSEL AND VIOLET SILK.
TAIL:	SILVER PHEASANT CREST OVER GOLDEN PHEASANT.
BUTT:	BLACK OSTRICH HERL.
BODY:	THREE EQUAL SECTIONS; THE FIRST OF PURPLE SILK, BUTTED BY SILVER PHEASANT CREST OVER GOLDEN PHEASANT AND BLACK HERL; THE SECOND OF RED SILK BUTTED BY BLACK HERL; THE THIRD OF YELLOW SILK.
RIB:	SILVER LACE.
THROAT:	RED-ORANGE HACKLE.
WINGS:	SILVER PHEASANT CREST OVER GOLDEN PHEASANT AND OUTSIDE 5 STRANDS OF ARGUS PHEASANT TAIL.
CHEEKS:	BRONZE HIMALAYAN MONAL PHEASANT NECK FEATHERS.
HEAD:	RED-ORANGE HERL.

AFRICAN GRAY
DESIGNED & TIED BY PAUL PTALIS 1997

HOOK: 6/0 MODIFIED HARRISON BY DAVE PARIS.
TAG: GOLD LACE AND PURPLE SILK.
TAIL: CHATTERER WITH PURPLE BASE (BACK TO BACK)
            OVER GOLDEN PHEASANT.
BUTT: LIGHT BLUE OSTRICH HERL.
BODY: FLAT SILVER TINSEL.
RIB: SALMON SILK BORDERED BY MEDIUM OVAL SILVER
            TINSEL.
THROAT: BUSTARD NECK HACKLE OVER COBALT VULTURINE
            GUINEA FOWL.
WINGS: AFRICAN GRAY PARROT AND A TOPPING.
SHOULDER: LAVENDER GUINEA FOWL.
CHEEKS: PARADISE TANAGER METALLIC RED-ORANGE RUMP
            FEATHER OVER PURPLE KINGFISHER.
HORNS: HYACINTH MACAW.

THE BRONZE PIRATE

ORIGINATED BY GEO. M. KELSON
THE "LAND AND WATER" SALMON FLIES, SERIES 3 1887-1888
INTERPRETED BY PAUL PTALIS 1993

HOOK: 6/0 ANTIQUE WM. BARTLEET.
TAG: SILVER TWIST.
TAIL: TOPPING.
BUTT: BLACK HERL.
BODY: SILVER TINSEL, RIBBED WITH SILVER TWIST, PARTIALLY
            BUTTED IN THREE EQUAL SECTIONS WITH IMPEYAN
            PHEASANT (CHEEK FEATHERS) INCREASING IN SIZE.
WINGS: IMPEYAN PHEASANT (DOUBLE, CREST)
            AND TWO TOPPINGS.
HEAD: BLACK HERL.

Comment: In order to tie this fly for a 6/0 presentation, blue feathers from the back of the pheasant were substituted for the crest feathers called for in the original pattern.

THE BRONZE PIRATE

Originated by F.L. Popham, Pattern per Geo. M. Kelson
"The Salmon Fly" 1895
Interpreted by Paul Ptalis 1996

HOOK: #4 ANTIQUE HARRISON BARTLEET, HOLLOW POINT
           SPROAT.
TAG: SILVER TWIST.
TAIL: TOPPING.
BUTT: BLACK HERL.
BODY: SILVER TINSEL, RIBBED WITH SILVER TWIST, PARTIALLY
           BUTTED IN THREE EQUAL SECTIONS WITH IMPEYAN
           PHEASANT (CHEEK FEATHERS) INCREASING IN SIZE.
WINGS: IMPEYAN PHEASANT (DOUBLE, CREST) AND
           TWO TOPPINGS.
HEAD: BLACK HERL.

BLUE CAPPED MACAW

A Variation of The Chatterer
Originated by Major Traherne, Pattern per Geo. M. Kelson
"The Salmon Fly" 1895
Interpreted By Paul Ptalis 1997

HOOK: 6/0 MODIFIED HARRISON BY D. PARIS.
TAG: FINE OVAL SILVER TINSEL AND ORANGE FLOSS.
TAIL: GOLDEN PHEASANT CREST.
BUTT: NATURAL BLACK OSTRICH.
BODY: TWO TURNS OF PURPLE FLOSS MAKING HEADWAY
           FOR NUMBERLESS SMALL BLUE CAPPED MACAW
           HEAD FEATHERS, CLOSELY PACKED ROUND THE
           REST OF THE BODY.
THROAT: BUSTARD NECK HACKLE.
WINGS: FOUR INDIAN CROW FEATHERS IN PAIRS
           (BACK TO BACK); WITH SIX TOPPINGS.
CHEEKS: METALLIC GREEN WEAVER.
HORNS: HYACINTH MACAW.

KINGFISHER

A Variation of The Chatterer
Originated by Major Traherne, Pattern per Geo. M. Kelson
"The Salmon Fly" 1895
Interpreted By Paul Ptalis 1997

HOOK: 6/0 MODIFIED HARRISON BY D. PARIS.
TAG: SILVER TINSEL (FINE OVAL) AND LIGHT ORANGE SILK.
TAIL: GOLDEN PHEASANT CREST.
BUTT: NATURAL BLACK OSTRICH.
BODY: THREE TURNS OF VIOLET SILK MAKING HEADWAY FOR
           NUMBERLESS SMALL BLUE FEATHERS FROM A
           KINGFISHER, CLOSELY PACKED ROUND THE REST OF
           THE BODY.
THROAT: BUSTARD NECK HACKLE.
WINGS: FOUR COCK-OF-THE-ROCK FEATHERS, IN PAIRS
           (BACK TO BACK), HAVING A POINT OF JAY FEATHER
           ON EACH SIDE, WITH FIVE OR SIX TOPPINGS.
HORNS: BLUE MACAW.

RED CAPPED LORI

A Variation of The Chatterer
Originated by Major Traherne, Pattern per Geo. M. Kelson
"The Salmon Fly" 1895
Interpreted By Paul Ptalis 1997

HOOK:	6/0 MODIFIED HARRISON BY D. PARIS.
TAG:	FINE OVAL SILVER TINSEL AND ORANGE FLOSS.
TAIL:	GOLDEN PHEASANT CREST.
BUTT:	NATURAL BLACK OSTRICH.
BODY:	TWO TURNS OF PURPLE FLOSS MAKING HEADWAY FOR NUMBERLESS SMALL RED CAPPED LORY HEAD FEATHERS, CLOSELY PACKED ROUND THE REST OF THE BODY.
THROAT:	BUSTARD NECK HACKLE.
WINGS:	FOUR COCK-OF-THE-ROCK FEATHERS IN PAIRS (BACK TO BACK); WITH SIX TOPPINGS.
HORNS:	HYACINTH MACAW.

RED CHEEKED MACAW

A Variation of The Chatterer
Originated by Major Traherne, Pattern per Geo. M. Kelson
"The Salmon Fly" 1895
Interpreted By Paul Ptalis 1997

HOOK: 6/0 MODIFIED HARRISON BY D. PARIS.
TAG: FINE OVAL SILVER TINSEL AND ORANGE FLOSS.
TAIL: GOLDEN PHEASANT CREST.
BUTT: NATURAL BLACK OSTRICH.
BODY: TWO TURNS OF YELLOW FLOSS MAKING HEADWAY
            FOR NUMBERLESS SMALL RED CHEEKED MACAW -
            GREEN HEAD FEATHERS, CLOSELY PACKED ROUND
            THE REST OF THE BODY.
THROAT: BUSTARD NECK HACKLE.
WINGS: FOUR INDIAN CROW FEATHERS IN PAIRS
            (BACK TO BACK), THE FIRST PAIR LONGER THAN
            THE SECOND; WITH SIX TOPPINGS.
HORNS: BLUE AND GOLD MACAW.

Sun Conour

A Variation of The Chatterer
Originated by Major Traherne, Pattern per Geo. M. Kelson
"The Salmon Fly" 1895
Interpreted By Paul Ptalis 1997

HOOK: 6/0 MODIFIED HARRISON BY D. PARIS.
TAG: FINE OVAL SILVER TINSEL AND RED FLOSS.
TAIL: GOLDEN PHEASANT CREST.
BUTT: NATURAL BLACK OSTRICH.
BODY: TWO TURNS OF BLUE FLOSS MAKING HEADWAY FOR NUMBERLESS SMALL SUN CONOUR BREAST FEATHERS, CLOSELY PACKED ROUND THE REST OF THE BODY.
THROAT: BUSTARD NECK HACKLE OVER COBALT VULTURINE GUINEA FOWL.
WINGS: FOUR COCK-OF-THE-ROCK FEATHERS IN PAIRS (BACK TO BACK); WITH SIX TOPPINGS.
HORNS: HYACINTH MACAW.

ECK'S ENGINE
DESIGNED & TIED BY PAUL PTALIS 1995

HOOK: 6/0 MODIFIED HARRISON BY D. PARIS.

TAG: FINE GOLD OVAL TINSEL AND RED SILK.

TAIL: GOLDEN PHEASANT.

BUTT: NATURAL BLACK OSTRICH.

BODY: IN TWO SECTIONS; THE FIRST THREE FIFTHS OF FLAT COPPER TINSEL, VIELED WITH GOLDEN PHEASANT CREST AND BUTTED WITH NATURAL BLACK OSTRICH. THE LAST TWO FIFTHS; YELLOW, TANGERINE AND RED/ORANGE SEAL'S FUR.

RIB: FIRST SECTION; SMALL OVAL SILVER TINSEL TIED COUNTER-CLOCKWISE. THE SECOND SECTION; SMALL OVAL SILVER TINSEL.

THROAT: RED/ORANGE OVER TANGERINE HACKLE.

WINGS: YELLOW, TANGERINE, ORANGE, SCARLET AND CRIMSON MARRIED TURKEY (3Y,1T,2Y,2T,1Y,3T,1O, 2T,2O,1T,3O,1S,2O,2S,1O, 3S,1C,2S,2C,1S,3C), AND A TOPPING.

CHEEKS: RIFLEBIRD OVER PITTA RUMP.

HORNS: SCARLET MACAW.

Comment: Designed and tied for my friend Rick Eck.

ELLIOT'S

DESIGNED & TIED BY PAUL PTALIS 1998

HOOK:	6/0 MODIFIED HARRISON BY D. PARIS.
TAG:	FINE OVAL SILVER TINSEL AND CRIMSON FLOSS.
TAIL:	GOLDEN PHEASANT CREST AND CHATTERER (BACK TO BACK).
BUTT:	NATURAL BLACK OSTRICH.
BODY:	THREE EQUAL SECTIONS; MEDIUM OVAL TINSEL BUTTED BY BLACK OSTRICH HERL.
RIB:	FINE OVAL SILVER TINSEL.
THROAT:	WIDGEON OVER ELLIOT'S BACK/RUMP FEATHER.
WINGS:	ELLIOT'S PHEASANT UNDER-TAIL COVERTS.
SHOULDER:	THREE ELLIOT'S COPPER NECK FEATHERS INCREASING IN SIZE.
CHEEKS:	METALLIC BLUE FROM PARADISE TANANGER.
HORNS:	AMHERST PHEASANT TAIL.

THE EMERALD PEACOCK

DESIGNED & TIED BY PAUL PTALIS 1995

HOOK:	8/0 MODIFIED HARRISON BY D. PARIS.
TAG:	GOLD TINSEL (FINE OVAL) AND PURPLE SILK.
TAIL:	GOLDEN PHEASANT CREST AND BLUE CHATTERER.
BUTT:	NATURAL CHARCOAL OSTRICH HERL.
BODY:	THREE EQUAL SECTIONS; THE FIRST TWO OF MACAW GREEN SILK, EACH HAVING TWO PEACOCK PHEASANT BACK TO BACK AND BELOW, AND EACH BUTTED WITH NATURAL BLACK OSTRICH HERL; THE LAST SECTION OF MACAW GREEN SILK.
RIB:	OVAL SILVER TINSEL (FINE).
THROAT:	FOUR PEACOCK PHEASANT IN TWO PAIRS (BACK TO BACK), THE OUTER PAIR SHORTER THAN THE INNER PAIR.
WINGS:	GREEN MACAW VEILED BY THREE PEACOCK PHEASANT IN SMALLER GRADUATED SIZES FROM THE BUTT TO THE HEAD OF THE FLY.
CHEEK:	FAIRY BLUE BIRD (V STYLE) AND CENTER BLUE CHATTERER.
TOPPING:	TWO GOLDEN PHEASANT CRESTS.
HORNS:	YELLOW AND GREEN MACAW.

Evan's Fancy

Designed & Tied By Paul Ptalis 1996

HOOK:	6/0 MODIFIED HARRISON BY D. PARIS.
TAG:	GOLD TINSEL (FINE OVAL) AND DARK BLUE SILK.
TAIL:	GOLDEN PHEASANT CREST AND A PAIR OF CHATTERER BACK TO BACK.
BUTT:	NATURAL BLACK OSTRICH.
BODY:	THREE EQUAL SECTIONS: THE FIRST TWO OF YELLOW AND BLUE SILK, A PAIR OF GREEN-TIPPED RED UNDER-TAIL LORIKEET COVERTS BACK TO BACK AND BELOW, BUTTED BY NATURAL BLACK OSTRICH; THE THIRD OF LIGHT GREEN SILK.
RIB:	GOLD TINSEL.
THROAT:	A PAIR OF GREEN-TIPPED RED UNDER-TAIL LORIKEET COVERTS BACK TO BACK.
WINGS:	SCARLET MACAW WITH GREEN TIP.
SHOULDER:	DARK RED MACAW.
SIDES:	FLAME-COLORED MINIVET OVER BLUE-STREAKED LORIKEET.
TOPPING:	GOLDEN PHEASANT CREST.
HORNS:	BLUE AND GOLD MACAW.

Comment: Designed and tied in honor of my son Evan.

FLOODTIDE

ORIGINATED BY GEO. M. KELSON
"THE SALMON FLY" 1895
INTERPRETED BY PAUL PTALIS 1996

HOOK: 7/0 ANTIQUE R. HARRISON, CELEBRATED DUBLIN
             LIMERICK.
TAG: FLAT SILVER TINSEL AND CRIMSON FLOSS.
TAIL: GOLDEN PHEASANT CREST AND SUMMER DUCK.
BUTT: NATURAL BLACK OSTRICH.
BODY: CANARY, YELLOW, DARK-ORANGE AND CRIMSON
             SEAL FUR.
RIB: FLAT SILVER AND SILVER LACE.
HACKLE: YELLOW EAGLE OVER THE DARK-ORANGE AND
             CRIMSON FUR.
THROAT: TWO TURNS OF DYED CRIMSON GUINEA FOWL.
WINGS: TWO JUNGLE COCK ENVELOPED BY TWO GOLDEN
             PHEASANT SWORDS; BUSTARD, AMHERST TAIL,
             YELLOW AND CRIMSON SWAN; TOPPING.
SIDES: JUNGLE COCK.
CHEEKS: JUNGLE POINTS.

Green Highlander

Originated by Major Grant, Pattern per Dr. T.E. Pryce-Tannatt
"How to Dress Salmon Flies" 1914
Interpreted By Paul Ptalis 1997

HOOK:	4/0 O. MUSTAD & SON, HOLLOW POINT SPROAT.
TAG:	SILVER TINSEL.
TAIL:	GOLDEN PHEASANT CREST AND BARRED SUMMER DUCK.
BUTT:	BLACK OSTRICH HERL.
BODY:	FIRST QUARTER, GOLDEN YELLOW FLOSS, REMAINDER BRIGHT GREEN SEAL'S FUR.
RIBS:	OVAL SILVER TINSEL.
HACKLE:	A GRASS-GREEN COCK'S HACKLE.
THROAT:	A LEMON COCK'S HACKLE.
WINGS:	MIXED GOLDEN PHEASANT TIPPET IN STRANDS, MARRIED SECTIONS OF YELLOW, ORANGE AND GREEN SWAN, FLORICAN, PEACOCK WING AND GOLDEN PHEASANT TAIL; OUTSIDE OF THIS, MARRIED SECTIONS OF TEAL AND BARRED SUMMER DUCK; NARROW SECTIONS OF BROWN MALLARD OVER AND A TOPPING.
SIDES:	JUNGLE COCK.
CHEEKS:	INDIAN CROW.
HORNS:	BLUE AND YELLOW MACAW.

GREY EAGLE

ORIGINATED BY MR. MURDOCH, PATTERN PER CAPTAIN J.H. HALE
"HOW TO TIE SALMON FLIES" 1892
INTERPRETED BY PAUL PTALIS 1997

HOOK: 7/0 ANTIQUE HARRISON'S SPRING STEEL SPROAT.
TAG: SILVER TWIST.
TAIL: TIP OF GOLDEN PHEASANT BREAST FEATHER.
BODY: LEMON-YELLOW, PALE-BLUE AND SCARLET SEAL FUR.
RIB: FLAT SILVER TINSEL.
HACKLE: GREY EAGLE.
THROAT: TEAL.
WINGS: GREY MOTTLED TURKEY, SET FLAT. (ORIGINAL PATTERN
            CALLS FOR BROWN MOTTLED TURKEY)

HARMONY

DESIGNED & TIED BY PAUL PTALIS 1996

HOOK:	8/0 MODIFIED HARRISON BY D. PARIS.
TAG:	GOLD TINSEL (FINE OVAL) AND DARK BLUE SILK.
TAIL:	GOLDEN PHEASANT CREST AND A PAIR OF KINGFISHER (BLUE WITH PURPLE BASE) BACK TO BACK.
BUTT:	NATURAL BLACK OSTRICH.
BODY:	THREE EQUAL SECTIONS: THE FIRST OF SALMON SILK BUTTED BY NATURAL BLACK OSTRICH; THE SECOND OF RED SILK BUTTED BY NATURAL BLACK OSTRICH; THE THIRD OF LIGHT GREEN SILK BUTTED BY NATURAL BLACK OSTRICH. A PAIR OF RED/ORANGE WITH YELLOW BASE UNDER-TAIL LORIKEET COVERTS BACK TO BACK AND BELOW AT BUTT OF EACH SECTION.
RIB:	GOLD TINSEL.
THROAT:	GREEN METALLIC WEAVER, OVER OF KINGFISHER (BLUE WITH PURPLE BASE), OVER PENNANT ROSELLA.
WINGS:	SCARLET MACAW WITH GREEN TIP.
SHOULDER:	PENNANT ROSELLA.
SIDES:	GREEN METALLIC WEAVER OVER OF KINGFISHER (BLUE WITH PURPLE BASE).
TOPPING:	GOLDEN PHEASANT CREST.
HORNS:	HYACINTH MACAW.

IBIS & MEARNS

DESIGNED & TIED BY PAUL PTALIS 1998

HOOK: 6/0 MODIFIED HARRISON BY D. PARIS.
TAG: FINE OVAL SILVER TINSEL, BLUE SILK THE SAME
           COLOR AS THE GIANT PITTA RUMP.
TAIL: PURPLE AND BLUE CHATTERER, BACK TO BACK, OVER
           GOLDEN PHEASANT CREST .
BUTT: NATURAL BLACK OSTRICH.
BODY: IN THREE SECTIONS; TWO FIFTHS, TWO FIFTHS AND
           ONE FIFTH EACH OF PURPLE SILK. THE FIRST TWO
           SECTIONS TERMINATING ON THE BOTTOM WITH
           MEARNS QUAIL (BACK TO BACK, GRADUATING IN SIZE)
           AND NATURAL BLACK OSTRICH.
RIB: FINE OVAL SILVER TINSEL.
THROAT: MEARNS QUAIL (BACK TO BACK).
WINGS: IBIS AND GOLDEN PHEASANT CREST.
SHOULDER: VULTURINE GUINEA FOWL BODY FEATHER.
CHEEKS: BLUE WITH GREEN BASE MACAW BODY FEATHER
           OVER GIANT PITTA RUMP.
HORNS: HYACINTH MACAW.

JK's Fault

Designed & Tied By Paul Ptalis 1999

HOOK:	7/0 WM. BARTLEET BY R. W. REINHOLD
TAG:	FINE GOLD OVAL TINSEL AND CRIMSON FLOSS.
TAIL:	GOLDEN PHEASANT CREST AND KINGFISHER DYED DARK BLUE (BACK TO BACK).
BUTT:	NATURAL BLACK OSTRICH.
BODY:	IN EQUAL SECTIONS; CANARY YELLOW, GOLDEN YELLOW, LIGHT ORANGE, ORANGE AND RED-ORANGE FLOSS.
RIB:	FINE GOLD OVAL TINSEL
THROAT:	A RED-ORANGE HACKLE OVER A TANGERINE HACKLE.
UNDERWING:	TWO RED-ORANGE HACKLES SANDWICHED BETWEEN TWO YELLOW HACKLES TIED IN UPSIDE-DOWN.
WINGS:	MARRIED YELLOW, LIGHT ORANGE, ORANGE, SCARLET AND CRIMSON TURKEY (PATTERN 3-2-1, 1-2-3-2-1, 1-2-3).
CHEEKS:	KINGFISHER DYED DARK BLUE OVER PENNANT ROSELLA.
TOPPING:	GOLDEN PHEASANT CREST.
HORNS:	SCARLET MACAW.

Comment: Designed and tied for my friend Al Coif.

JUSTIN'S FANCY

DESIGNED & TIED BY PAUL PTALIS 1993

HOOK:	8/0 PARTRIDGE, ADLINGTON & HUTCHINSON.
TAG:	FINE GOLD OVAL TINSEL PURPLE AND YELLOW SILK.
TAIL:	GOLDEN PHEASANT, YELLOW BORDERED BY PURPLE SWAN- MARRIED, AND KINGFISHER.
BUTT:	PURPLE OSTRICH.
BODY:	IN TWO SECTIONS; THE FIRST TWO FIFTHS OF EMBOSSED GOLD TINSEL, BUTTED WITH PURPLE OSTRICH. THE LAST THREE FIFTHS; PURPLE SILK.
RIB:	FIRST SECTION; DARK PURPLE SILK BORDERED BY SMALL OVAL SILVER TINSEL. THE SECOND SECTION; YELLOW SILK BORDERED BY SMALL OVAL SILVER TINSEL
THROAT:	GALLENA OVER PURPLE OVER LIGHT BLUE HACKLE.
WINGS:	PALAWAN PEACOCK PHEASANT AND TWO TOPPINGS.
CHEEKS:	PEACOCK NECK FEATHER OVER CRIMSON LORIKEET.
HEAD:	PURPLE OSTRICH.

Comment: Designed and tied for my friend Justin Krul.

Moon and Stars

Originated by Ken Sawada
"Classic Salmon fly Dressing" 1994
Interpreted by Paul Ptalis 1997

HOOK: 6/0 O. MUSTAD & SON, HOLLOW POINT SPROAT.

TAG: SILVER WIRE, PURPLE FLOSS, SILVER ROUND TINSEL AND REDDISH PURPLE FLOSS.

TAIL: LOWER HALF; LAVENDER AND GALLENA QUILL. UPPER HALF; PURPLE AND GALLENA QUILL. ALL TWO STRANDS EACH AND MARRIED TOGETHER.

BUTT: DARK BLUE HERL.

BODY: THREE TURNS OF PURPLE, REMAINDER BLACK FLOSS.

RIBS: PURPLE FLOSS WITH FINE SILVER LACE AT EACH SIDE.

HACKLE: DARK BLUE.

THROAT: FROM PEACOCK PHEASANT SPECKLED TAIL FEATHER.

WINGS: TWO STRANDS OF BLUE MACAW, ONE STRAND OF BLACK AND WHITE BUSTARD AND PURPLE QUILL. MARRIED TOGETHER TO FORM UNDERWING; MARRIED WITH FINE STRANDS OF ARGUS PHEASANT TAIL AND DARK BLUE QUILL TO FORM UPPER WING.

SIDES: MARRIED WITH SINGLE STRAND OF BLUE MACAW, TWO STRANDS EACH OF YELLOW AND BLACK GOOSE.

HORNS: BLUE MACAW.

Comment: A superb Sawada pattern illustrating "flow."

THE POPHAM

ORIGINATED BY F. L. POPHAM, PATTERN PER GEO. M. KELSON
"THE SALMON FLY" 1895
INTERPRETED BY PAUL PTALIS 1996

HOOK: 6/0 WM. BARTLEET BY R. W. REINHOLD.
TAG: GOLD TWIST.
TAIL: GOLDEN PHEASANT CREST AND INDIAN CROW.
BUTT: NATURAL BLACK OSTRICH.
BODY: IN THREE EQUAL SECTIONS, EACH TERMINATING WITH A BLACK HERL BUTT. THE FIRST OF DARK RED-ORANGE SILK, RIBBED WITH FINE GOLD TINSEL HAVING INDIAN CROW ABOVE AND BELOW; THE SECOND, YELLOW SILK WITH SIMILAR RIBBING AND CROW FEATHERS AS BEFORE; THE THIRD OF LIGHT BLUE SILK AND SILVER RIBBING WITH THE INDIAN CROW REPEATED.
THROAT: JAY.
WINGS: TIPPET, TEAL, GALLINA, GOLDEN PHEASANT TAIL, PARROT LIGHT BROWN MOTTLED TURKEY, BUSTARD, RED MACAW, YELLOW MACAW, WITH TWO STRIPS OF MALLARD ABOVE AND A TOPPING.
CHEEKS: BLUE CHATTERER.
HORNS: BLUE MACAW.

THE POPHAM

ORIGINATED BY F. L. POPHAM, PATTERN PER GEO. M. KELSON
"THE SALMON FLY" 1895
INTERPRETED BY PAUL PTALIS 1998

HOOK:	7/0 WM. BARTLEET BY R. W. REINHOLD.
TAG:	GOLD TWIST.
TAIL:	GOLDEN PHEASANT CREST AND INDIAN CROW.
BUTT:	NATURAL BLACK OSTRICH.
BODY:	IN THREE EQUAL SECTIONS, EACH TERMINATING WITH A BLACK HERL BUTT. THE FIRST OF DARK RED-ORANGE SILK, RIBBED WITH FINE GOLD TINSEL HAVING INDIAN CROW ABOVE AND BELOW; THE SECOND, YELLOW SILK WITH SIMILAR RIBBING AND CROW FEATHERS AS BEFORE; THE THIRD OF LIGHT BLUE SILK AND SILVER RIBBING WITH THE INDIAN CROW REPEATED.
THROAT:	JAY.
WINGS:	TIPPET, TEAL, GALLINA, GOLDEN PHEASANT TAIL, PARROT LIGHT BROWN MOTTLED TURKEY, BUSTARD, RED MACAW, YELLOW MACAW, WITH TWO STRIPS OF MALLARD ABOVE AND A TOPPING..
CHEEKS:	BLUE CHATTERER.
HORNS:	BLUE MACAW.

PRIMARY DIRECTION

DESIGNED & TIED BY PAUL PTALIS 1995

HOOK: 7/0 ANTIQUE R. HARRISON, CELEBRATED DUBLIN
              LIMERICK.
TAG: GOLD OVAL TINSEL (FINE), PURPLE AND YELLOW SILK.
TAIL: GOLDEN PHEASANT CREST AND PURPLE CHATTERER.
BUTT: NATURAL BLACK OSTRICH HERL.
BODY: THREE EQUAL SECTIONS; THE FIRST OF BLUE SILK,
              MARRIED SECTIONS OF KENYA CRESTED GUINEA
              FOWL AND BLUE SWAN ABOVE AND BELOW AND
              BUTTED WITH NATURAL BLACK OSTRICH HERL. THE
              SECOND SECTION THE SAME EXCEPT OF RED SILK.
              THE THIRD SECTION OF YELLOW SILK.
RIB: VERY FINE GOLD OVAL TINSEL.
THROAT: MARRIED SECTIONS OF KENYA CRESTED GUINEA
              FOWL AND YELLOW SWAN VEILED BY JUNGLE COCK.
UNDERWING: MARRIED SECTIONS OF KENYA CRESTED GUINEA
              FOWL AND YELLOW SWAN.
WINGS: MARRIED YELLOW, RED, AND BLUE DYED FLORICAN,
              AND SPECKLED BUSTARD AS FOLLOWS: 4 SECTIONS
              (1Y,1R,1B, 2SB), 3Y, 1B, 2R, 1B.
SIDES: JUNGLE COCK.
CHEEKS: PURPLE CHATTERER OVER KINGFISHER
TOPPING: GOLDEN PHEASANT CREST.
HORNS: SCARLET MACAW.

REGAL KING

Designed & Tied By Paul Ptalis 1997

HOOK:	6/0 MODIFIED HARRISON BY D. PARIS.
TAG:	FINE GOLD OVAL TINSEL AND PURPLE SILK.
TAIL:	KINGFISHER (BACK TO BACK) OVER GOLDEN PHEASANT.
BUTT:	NATURAL OSTRICH HERL.
BODY:	EMBOSSED GOLD TINSEL (BACKGROUND ANTIQUED).
RIB:	RED SILK BORDERED BY FINE OVAL SILVER TINSEL.
THROAT:	PURPLE GUINEA FOWL OVER RED HACKLE.
WINGS:	GRAY PEACOCK PHEASANT AND A TOPPING.
SHOULDER:	RED UNDER TAIL COVERT FROM A BLUE STREAKED LORIKEET.
CHEEKS:	KINGFISHER OVER BLUE PEACOCK NECK FEATHER.
HORNS:	SCARLET MACAW.

Roy G. Biv

Designed & Tied By Paul Ptalis 1996

HOOK: 6/0 WM. BARTLEET BY R. W. REINHOLD.
TAG: GOLD OVAL TINSEL (FINE), RED SILK.
TAIL: GOLDEN PHEASANT CREST AND KINGFISHER BACK
             TO BACK.
BUTT: BLACK OSTRICH HERL.
BODY: FIVE EQUAL SECTIONS OF SILK; ORANGE, YELLOW,
             GREEN, BLUE, INDIGO.
RIB: GOLD OVAL TINSEL (FINE).
THROAT: ORANGE-RED HACKLE OVER TANGERINE.
UNDERWING: VULTURINE GUINEA FOWL.
WINGS: MARRIED SECTIONS OF DYED TURKEY; INDIGO,
             BLUE, GREEN, YELLOW, ORANGE, RED: SEPARATED
             AND BORDERED BY BLACK CAPERCAILLIE TAIL.
CHEEKS: KINGFISHER OVER TROGAN.
TOPPING: GOLDEN PHEASANT CREST.
HORNS: HYACINTH MACAW.

Comment: I tie this fly in several variations: the underwing using pheasant swords
(red, orange, yellow), the tail veilings using barred wood duck and Ibis, the throat using
cobalt vulturine guinea fowl, and several reverse order variations of wing and body
(but always in the roygbiv or vibgyor order).

SARAH'S FANCY

DESIGNED & TIED BY PAUL PTALIS 1994

HOOK:	4/0 PARTRIDGE, ADLINGTON & HUTCHINSON.
TAG:	GOLD TINSEL (FINE OVAL) AND DARK BLUE SILK.
TAIL:	GOLDEN PHEASANT CREST AND A PAIR OF ORANGE FEATHERS FROM THE JENDAYA PARAKEET.
BUTT:	NATURAL BLACK OSTRICH.
BODY:	THREE EQUAL SECTIONS: THE FIRST TWO OF LIGHT GREEN SILK TO MATCH WING, A PAIR OF GREEN JENDAYA WITH CHARCOAL CENTERS BACK TO BACK AND BELOW, BUTTED BY NATURAL BLACK OSTRICH; THE THIRD OF LIGHT GREEN SILK.
RIB:	GOLD TINSEL.
THROAT:	A PAIR OF GREEN JENDAYA WITH CHARCOAL CENTERS BACK TO BACK.
WINGS:	LIGHT GREEN MACAW COVERLETS WITH IRIDESCENT BLUE-GREEN TINGE.
SHOULDER:	KENYA CRESTED GUINEA FOWL.
SIDES:	YELLOW GREEN WITH ORANGE CENTER OVER LIGHT BLUE, BOTH FROM JENDAYA PARAKEET.
TOPPING:	GOLDEN PHEASANT CREST.
HORNS:	YELLOW AND GREEN MACAW.

Comment: Designed and tied in honor of my daughter Sarah.

THE SCARLET GEM

A VARIATION OF THE EMERALD GEM
ORIGINATED BY MAJOR TRAHERNE, "THE FISHING GAZETTE" 1884
INTERPRETED BY PAUL PTALIS 1994

HOOK: 6/0 PARTRIDGE, ADLINGTON & HUTCHINSON.
TAG: GOLD TWIST AND PURPLE SILK.
TAIL: GOLDEN PHEASANT CREST.
BUTT: BLACK OSTRICH HERL.
BODY: GOLD TINSEL IN THREE EQUAL SECTIONS, BUTTED
           BY BLACK OSTRICH HERL.
HACKLE: BLUE STREAKED LORIKEET AT THE TERMINATION OF
           EACH DIVISION.
WINGS: GOLDEN PHEASANT CREST.
HORNS: SCARLET MACAW.

SCARLET QUEEN

DESIGNED & TIED BY PAUL PTALIS 1998

HOOK:	6/0 MODIFIED HARRISON BY D. PARIS.
TAG:	FINE GOLD OVAL TINSEL AND DARK BLUE SILK.
TAIL:	IBIS OVER GOLDEN PHEASANT.
BUTT:	NATURAL OSTRICH HERL.
BODY:	RED SILK.
RIB:	DARK BLUE SILK BORDERED BY FINE GOLD OVAL TINSEL.
THROAT:	DARK BLUE OVER LIGHT BLUE HACKLE.
WINGS:	SCARLET MACAW SECONDARIES WITH RED STEM AND BLUE/GREEN TIPS AND A TOPPING.
SHOULDER:	SCARLET MACAW BODY FEATHER.
CHEEKS:	TROGON.
HORNS:	SCARLET MACAW.

SHEWEY'S MARABOU BLUE

DESIGNED & TIED BY PAUL PTALIS 1996

HOOK:	6/0 MODIFIED HARRISON BY D. PARIS.
TAG:	FINE GOLD OVAL TINSEL AND ORANGE SILK.
TAIL:	GOLDEN PHEASANT CREST, IBIS AND CHATTERER.
BUTT:	NATURAL BLACK OSTRICH.
BODY:	IN TWO EQUAL SECTIONS: THE FIRST OF DARK BLUE SILK RIBBED WITH SILVER TWIST; THE SECOND SECTION OF LIGHT BLUE SEAL FUR RIBBED WITH SILVER TWIST.
THROAT:	JOHN SHEWEY'S LIGHT BLUE MARABOU WITH DARK BLUE TIPS UNDER ORANGE MARABOU WITH PURPLE TIPS.
WINGS:	MARRIED ORANGE, KINGFISHER BLUE, BLUE, AND PURPLE TURKEY AS FOLLOWS: (3O,1LB,2O,2LB,2O, 1LB,1B,1LB,1O,2LB,2B, 3LB,3B,1P,1LB,1B,2P, 2B,3P,2B,5P) AND A TOPPING.
SHOULDER:	BLUE-GREEN PEACOCK NECK FEATHER.
CHEEKS:	FLAME-COLORED MINIVET.
HORNS:	ORANGE DYED AMHERST TAIL.

Comment: Besides being known as an outstanding writer and fisherman, John Shewey's skill and creativity with respect to dying fly tying materials is exceptional. All the dyed materials used in this fly are John's. Of special note is the marabou used for the throat, the contrasting color dye is hand rolled on each feather allowing the tier to create interesting patterns.

Spring Fancy

Designed & Tied By Paul Ptalis 1997

HOOK:	6/0 MODIFIED HARRISON BY D. PARIS.
TAG:	FINE GOLD OVAL TINSEL AND DARK BLUE SILK.
TAIL:	GOLDEN PHEASANT CREST AND TWO GREEN METALLIC WEAVER (BACK TO BACK).
BUTT:	NATURAL BLACK OSTRICH.
BODY:	IN FIVE EQUAL DIVISIONS: LIGHT GREEN, MEDIUM GREEN, BLUE-GREEN, LIGHT BLUE AND DARK BLUE SILK.
RIB:	FINE FLAT GOLD TINSEL FOLLOWED BY FINE OVAL SILVER TINSEL.
THROAT:	LIGHT GREEN HACKLE AND KENYA CRESTED GUINEA FOWL.
WINGS:	AN UNDERWING OF VULTURINE GUINEA FOWL. MARRIED YELLOW, GREEN, LIGHT BLUE AND BLUE TURKEY AS FOLLOWS; (3Y,1G,2Y,2G,1Y,3G,1LB,2G, 2LB,1G,3LB,1B,2LB,2B,1LB,3B), AND A TOPPING.
CHEEKS:	BLUE CHATTERER OVER PITTA RUMP.
HORNS:	BLUE AND YELLOW MACAW.

Tippetiwitchet

Originated by Major Traherne, "The Fishing Gazette" 1884
Interpreted By Paul Ptalis 1996

HOOK: 8/0 MODIFIED HARRISON BY D. PARIS.

TAG: SILVER TWIST, AND LIGHT BLUE SILK THE SAME COLOR AS A LIGHT BLUE CHATTERER.

TAIL: GOLDEN PHEASANT CREST.

BUTT: NATURAL BLACK OSTRICH.

BODY: IN FIVE EQUAL DIVISIONS, EACH TERMINATING WITH A BLACK HERL BUTT. THERE ARE FOUR TIPPETS; TWO (BACK TO BACK) TIED IN TOP AND BOTTOM OF EVERY SECTION OVER THE GOLDEN FLOSS WHICH, SILK IS THE SAME SHADE AS THE GOLDEN TOPPINGS.

RIB: OVAL TINSEL.

THROAT: BLUE CHATTERER.

WINGS: FIVE OR SIX TOPPINGS.

CHEEKS: BLUE CHATTERER.

HORNS: BLUE MACAW.

THE TORRISH

KELSON ATTRIBUTES THE TORRISH TO RADCLIFFE; GIMBLE, TO DONALD ROSS,
KEEPER AT TORRISH ON THAT RIVER, PATTERN PER BUCHLAND AND OGLEBY,
"A GUIDE TO SALMON FLIES," 1990
INTERPRETED BY PAUL PTALIS 1996

HOOK: 6/0 MODIFIED HARRISON BY D. PARIS.
TAG: SILVER TINSEL AND GOLDEN YELLOW FLOSS.
TAIL: GOLDEN PHEASANT CREST AND TIPPET.
BUTT: NATURAL BLACK OSTRICH.
BODY: IN TWO EQUAL PARTS OF OVAL SILVER TINSEL,
             BUTTED WITH INDIAN CROW AND BLACK OSTRICH
             HERL; THE FRONT SECTION PALMERED WITH
             YELLOW HACKLE.
THROAT: A RED-ORANGE HACKLE.
WINGS: TWO STRIPS OF BLACK TURKEY WHITE TIPPED, TEAL,
             SCARLET, YELLOW AND ORANGE SWAN, BUSTARD,
             FLORICAN, AND GOLDEN PHEASANT TAIL; OUTSIDE
             OF WHICH ARE MARRIED NARROW STRIPS OF PINTAIL
             AND BARRED SUMMER WOOD DUCK; OUTSIDE OF
             WHICH ARE NARROW STRIPS OF BROWN MALLARD.
CHEEKS: JUNGLE COCK AND INDIAN CROW.
TOPPING: GOLDEN PHEASANT CREST.
HORNS: BLUE AND YELLOW MACAW.

Yellow Eagle

Originated by Mr. Brown, Pattern per Captain Hale
"How to Tie Salmon flies," 1919 Edition
Interpreted By Paul Ptalis 1997

HOOK:	7/0 ANTIQUE HARRISON'S SPRING STEEL SPROAT.
TAG:	FLAT SILVER TINSEL.
TAIL:	TIP OF GOLDEN PHEASANT BREAST FEATHER.
BODY:	LEMON-YELLOW, PALE-BLUE AND SCARLET SEAL FUR.
RIB:	FLAT SILVER TINSEL.
HACKLE:	EAGLE DYED YELLOW.
THROAT:	TEAL.
WINGS:	GREY MOTTLED TURKEY, SET FLAT.

HOOKS

The antique section includes original hooks from the 19th and early 20th centuries. The hooks shown depict a relatively broad representation of the originals. They have been available for purchase at the fly fishing shows and through collectors over the past several years. This section is intended to serve as a reference for those who are not familiar with the originals. The hooks are shown actual-size. Each year their availability decreases, contributing to their ever-increasing cost. Most tiers no longer use these hooks to tie exhibition flies, favoring to keep their antique collection in tact.

The contemporary section includes exhibition quality replicas (some with modifications) of the originals that are available today. They are all hand made by, who I consider to be, the contemporary "masters." They include such notables as Ron W. Reinhold, Ray Smith, and Eugene Sunday.

A little about hook points, barbs and Dee hooks :
(Excerpts of information contained in the R.W. Reinhold catalog.)

Because antique hooks were all handmade, a most notable aspect about them is that the points are mostly different. Even in a box of a hundred of the same model, the points vary from one to the next.

Dublin points ("**Dublin Limerick**," or "**Improved Limerick**") are the most elegant. Dublin points have a subtle "S" curve on the surface facing the shank. The majority of exhibition flies tied today are tied on hooks with this point mainly because of its soothing graceful line and its contribution to the "flow" of the fly.

Hollow points are also popular with lots of character. They look like a sliver of crescent moon on the end of the hook bend. They have a real "fish hook look," made for the raw business of catching fish. In their day hollow points were regarded as the highest quality hooks available, due to the inordinate amount of hand filing required to make them.

Harpoon points are predominant on many antique hooks, but are very inconsistent in their size and shape. Nonetheless, they have their charm, probably because of their hint of crude efficiency. They are easier to grind than hollow points or Dublins, and appear to have been the predominant choice for fast production in the 19th century.

Round points are reflective of the machining techniques of the modern industrial age. These points are typically not stylish, they generally have a stubby, kicked-up barb and a crudely-ground conical point that resembles the tip of a low-quality needle. Characteristically, the finish is nearly flat black. The nostalgia and charm of early handmade hooks is eliminated. Although they are available at low cost, all sense of the grand traditions and sophistication of classic tying is generally perceived to be lost on hooks with round points.

Barbs run the gamut from beautifully graceful crescents to unsightly sharp humps. The highest quality hooks will have moderately long, polished barbs and, frequently, gutters. A **Gutter** is a shallow triangular trough that is filed or ground tangent to the barb at its base, and extends down into the base of the point. Gutters cause the barb to appear longer and more elegant, and incorporating them cleans up ragged edges on barbs.

Dee hooks are long shank, heavy wire hooks originally developed for use in the fast, heavy water of the River Dee in Scotland. Any hook labeled a Dee simply means it has extra length (not necessarily weight) characteristic of those originally used in Scotland.

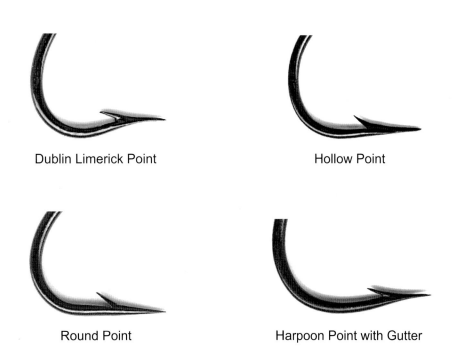

Dublin Limerick Point	Hollow Point
Round Point	Harpoon Point with Gutter

Ron Reinhold produces hooks of unusual quality in terms of both the finish and attention to detail compared to the originals. He offers a variety of bend styles and point styles in a multitude of sizes with several finishes. This is important, especially for the salmon fly tier who wants to tie on smaller quality hooks and/or may not have the materials to tie on hooks 4/0 and larger. His hooks are readily available compared to the other contemporary hook makers. He also makes hooks on a special order, custom basis, to accommodate any modifications desired by the tier. Ron's catalog is available from R.W. Reinhold Co. 44446 Westridge Drive, Williamsburg, Michigan 49690 – (231) 938-3229 or English Angling Trappings @ (203) 746-4121.

ANTIQUE HOOKS

R. WILLIS & SONS
CIRCA 1920
BRONZE JAPANNED

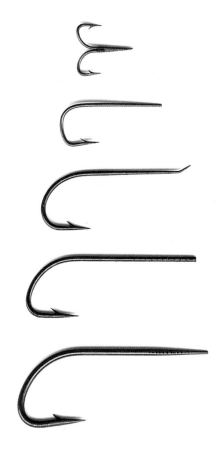

Antique Hooks

Wm. Bartleet & Sons
Fine Wire Limerick

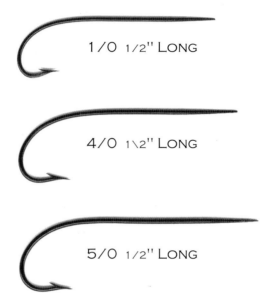

1/0 1/2" Long

4/0 1\2" Long

5/0 1/2" Long

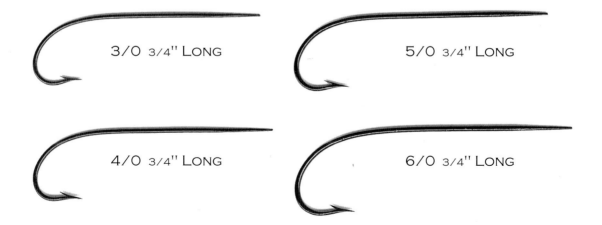

3/0 3/4" Long

5/0 3/4" Long

4/0 3/4" Long

6/0 3/4" Long

ANTIQUE HOOKS

R. HARRISON
CELEBRATED DUBLIN LIMERICK

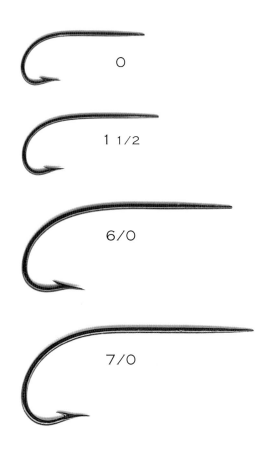

0

1 1/2

6/0

7/0

WM. BARTLEET & SONS
LIMERICK

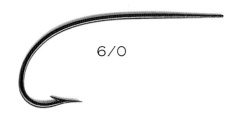

6/0

Antique Hooks

R. Harrison Bartleet & Co.
Celebrated Spring Steel Sproat

6/0

7/0

Pennell's Sproat
X Heavy Wire

6/0

Adlington
Round Bend

6/0

ANTIQUE HOOKS

H. MILLWARD
LIMERICK

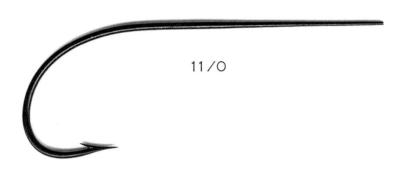

11/0

LOW WATER SALMON HOOK
CIRCA PRE-WWII

8/0

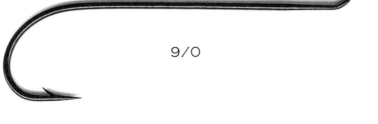

9/0

10/0

Antique Hooks

Edgar Sealey & Sons
Hollow Point Sproat

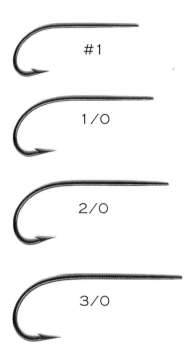

#1

1/0

2/0

3/0

Francis Francis
Plate #13 Carlisle Bend

Allcock
Limerick

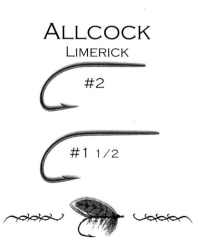

#2

#1 1/2

Antique Hooks

R. Harrison Bartleet & Co.
Limerick

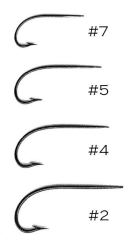

#7

#5

#4

#2

Harrison Bartleet's
Hollow Point
Sproat Bend

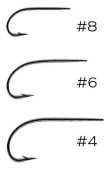

#8

#6

#4

Mustad #3450
Kinsey Hook

#16

Antique Hooks

Mustad #3899
Fine Wire Sproat
Hollow Point

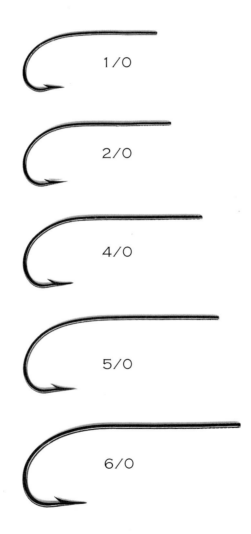

1/0

2/0

4/0

5/0

6/0

CONTEMPORARY HOOKS
BY
R.W. REINHOLD

CONTEMPORARY HOOKS
HOOK MAKER: R.W. REINHOLD

WM. BARTLEET & SONS

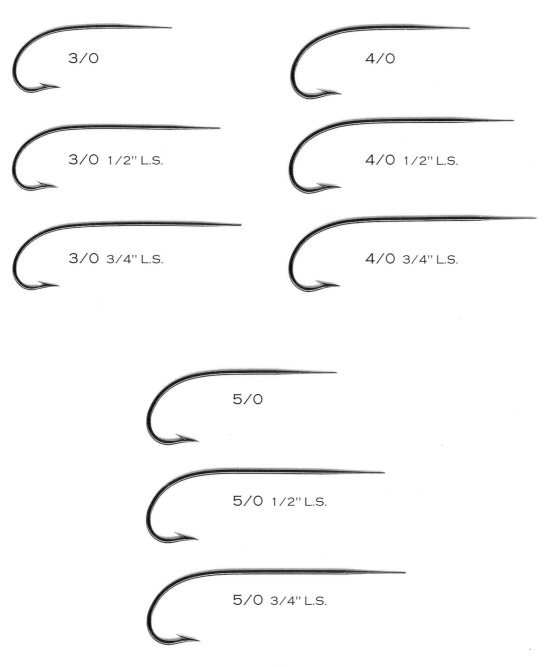

3/0

4/0

3/0 1/2" L.S.

4/0 1/2" L.S.

3/0 3/4" L.S.

4/0 3/4" L.S.

5/0

5/0 1/2" L.S.

5/0 3/4" L.S.

CONTEMPORARY HOOKS
HOOK MAKER: R.W. REINHOLD

HARRISON HOLLOW POINT

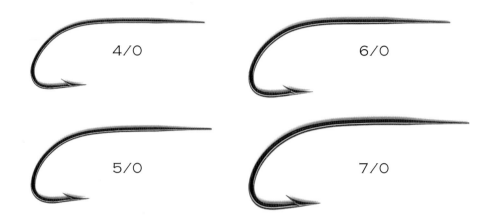

4/0

6/0

5/0

7/0

NOBLE HB

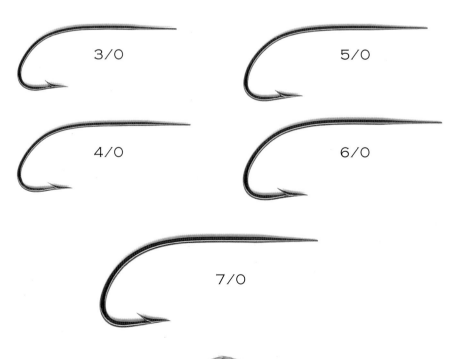

3/0

5/0

4/0

6/0

7/0

CONTEMPORARY HOOKS
HOOK MAKER: R.W. REINHOLD

PHILLIPS LIMERICK

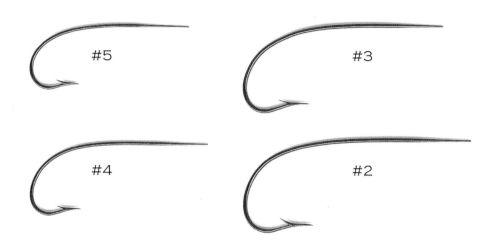

#5

#3

#4

#2

NOBLE P

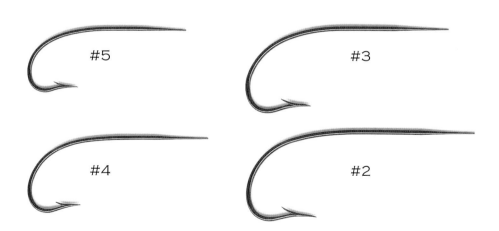

#5

#3

#4

#2

Contemporary Hooks
Hook Maker: R.W. Reinhold

Wm. Bartleet

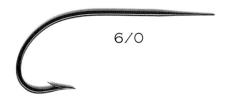

6/0

7/0

Droughtwater Dee

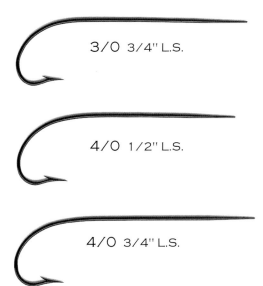

3/0 3/4" L.S.

4/0 1/2" L.S.

4/0 3/4" L.S.

Contemporary Hooks
Hook Maker: R.W. Reinhold

T.E. Pryce-Tannatt
Group A

2 1/4"

2 3/4"

Harrison Bartleet

7/0

7/0 XL

Millward Bartleet

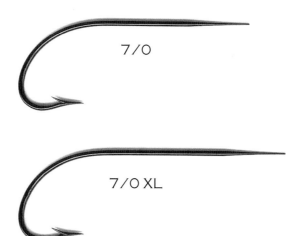

3/0

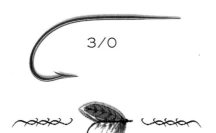

Contemporary Hooks
Hook Maker: R.W. Reinhold

Noble S

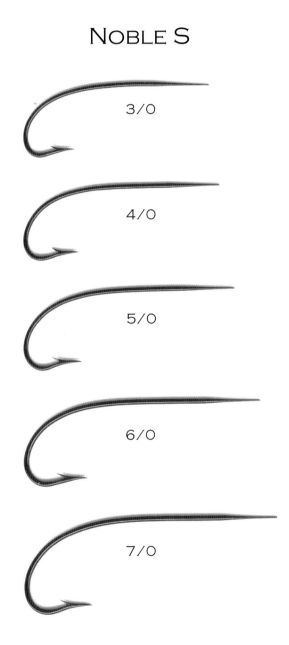

3/0

4/0

5/0

6/0

7/0

CONTEMPORARY HOOKS
BY
RAY SMITH

Contemporary Hooks

Hook Maker: Ray Smith

Wm. Bartleet & Sons
Limerick

1/0

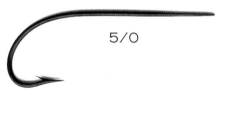

3/0

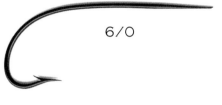

4/0

5/0

6/0

7/0

Contemporary Hooks
Hook Maker: Ray Smith

Wm. Bartleet
Limerick

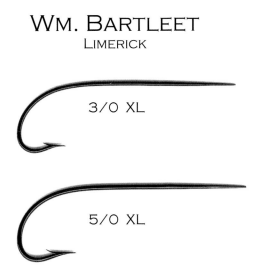

3/0 XL

5/0 XL

Harrison
Celebrated Limerick

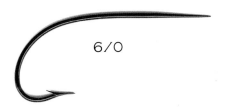

6/0

CONTEMPORARY HOOKS
HOOK MAKER: RAY SMITH

PHILLIPS OF DUBLIN

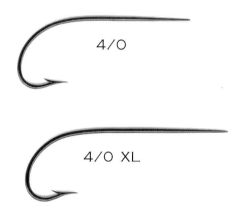

4/0

4/0 XL

PRYCE-TANNATT RATIONAL

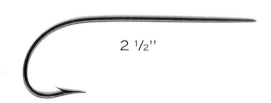

2 ½"

CONTEMPORARY HOOKS
BY
EUGENE SUNDAY

CONTEMPORARY HOOKS

HOOK MAKER: EUGENE SUNDAY

WM. BARTLEET & SONS

LIMERICK

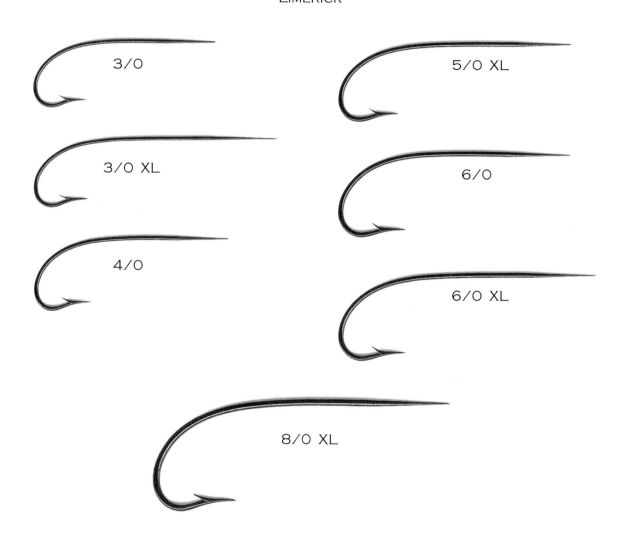

3/0

5/0 XL

3/0 XL

6/0

4/0

6/0 XL

8/0 XL

Contemporary Hooks
Hook Maker: Eugene Sunday

MADDEN
Celebrated Limerick

3/0

3/0 XL

5/0 XL

7/0 XL

HARRISON
Hollow Point Limerick

4/0 XL

4/0 2XL

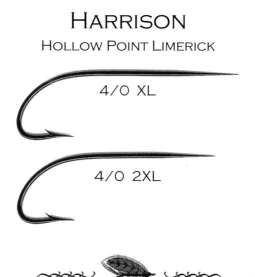

CONTEMPORARY HOOKS
HOOK MAKER: EUGENE SUNDAY

MILLWARD

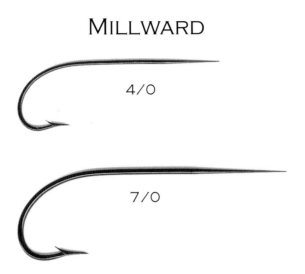

4/0

7/0

MATTHEW'S
SUPERFINE FORGED IRON

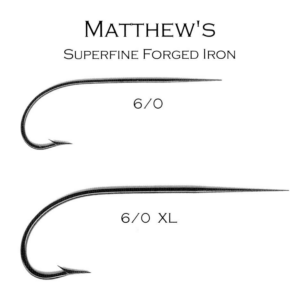

6/0

6/0 XL

NOTES

NOTES

NOTES

NOTES